S0-CBG-599

A PRAIRIE COULEE

A PRAIRIE COULEE

THOMAS WILLOCK

LONE
PINE

Copyright © 1990 by Thomas Willock

All rights reserved. No part of this work covered by the copyrights hereon may be reproduced or used in any form or by any means - graphic, electronic or mechanical - without the prior written permission of the publisher, except for reviewers who may quote brief passages.

Any request for photocopying, recording, taping or information storage and retrieval systems of any part of this book shall be directed in writing to the Canadian Reprography Collective, 379 Adelaide Street West, Suite M1, Toronto, Ontario M5V 1S5.

The Publisher:
Lone Pine Publishing
#206 10426-81 Avenue
Edmonton, Alberta, Canada
T6E 1X5

The author gratefully acknowledges financial assistance toward the preparation of this manuscript from the Fish and Wildlife Division of Alberta Forestry, Lands and Wildlife.

The publisher gratefully acknowledges the assistance of the Federal Department of Communications, Alberta Culture and Multiculturalism, the Canada Council, and the Alberta Foundation for the Literary Arts in the publication of this book.

Canadian Cataloguing in Publication Data

Willock, Tom, 1943-
   A prairie coulee

   Bibliography: p.88
   ISBN 0-919433-56-1

   1. Coulee ecology - Prairie Provinces. 2. Coulee ecology - Great Plains. 3. Grassland ecology - Prairie Provinces. 4. Grassland ecology - Great Plains. 5. Prairie ecology - Prairie Provinces. 6. Prairie ecology - Great Plains. I. Title.
QH541.5.P7W54 1990 574.5'2643'0971
                              C88-091464-5

Cover photos: Thomas Willock
Cover design: Yuet Chan
Editorial: Mary Walters Riskin, Jane Spalding
Layout: Yuet Chan
Photography: Thomas Willock
Printing: Quality Color Press Inc.

for Phyllis, Brian and Elaine

AUGUSTANA UNIVERSITY COLLEGE
LIBRARY

*We shall not cease from exploration
and the end of all our exploring
will be to arrive where we started
and know the place for the first time.*

— T.S. Eliot

contents

list of
illustrations

The following are black and white illustrations:

acknowledgements

OVER THE YEARS, the voices of many friends have encouraged my understanding of the prairie landscape. Coffee-shop conversations, discussions through the window of a half-ton, a hundred books read and, except for an occasional word or a phrase, forgotten; all have contributed to my impressions of the prairie. To all of those authors and friends I am grateful.

Among the works used more directly, Lewin's (1963) paper on the herpetofauna of southeastern Alberta was used as a basic guide to the amphibians and reptiles included. A.C. Budd and K.F. Best (1964), Lewin (1963), Kuijt (1972), and Cormack (1967) were consulted for information and selection of plant species. Godfrey (1966) and W.R. Salt and A.W. Wilk (1958) were used for information in the chapter on birds and much of the information in the chapter on mammals was obtained from Soper (1964) or Banfield (1974). W.B. Scott and E.J. Crossman (1973), D.E. McAllister and E.J. Crossman (1973) and M.J. Paetz and J.S. Nelson (1970) were consulted for information on fishes. The works of Durward L. Allen (1967), David F. Costello (1969) and W.C. Harty, et al (1967), especially the first two, were blatantly used throughout as fine sources of general natural history material on North American grasslands. The ecological concepts presented follow the third edition (1971) of Eugene P. Odum's *Fundamentals of Ecology* with additional information from S.C. Kendeigh (1961). Two works to which I am immensely indebted for their spirit and sensitivity are Wallace Stegner's *Wolf Willow*

(1955) and Aldo Leopold's *A Sand County Almanac* (1949).

I would like to thank Dr. Eric Mokosch and Dr. Chester Beaty, University of Lethbridge and Messrs. Dennis McDonald and Norman Gaelich, formerly of the Extension Services Branch, Fish and Wildlife Division, Alberta Recreation, Parks and Wildlife, for their cooperation, comments and guidance. Also, Dr. Luke Stebbins and other members of the faculty of the University of Lethbridge Department of Biological Sciences for their interest and support. Thanks go to Dr. Job Kuijt for his patient editing of the manuscript, to Dr. Hope Johnson for her general review as well as her comments on the geology of the area, to Monty Reid for his perceptive and worthwhile comments and to Mary Walters Riskin, editor-in-chief at Lone Pine for her encouragement, comments and patience. I would like to express my appreciation to Mr. and Mrs. Ed Turner and the many other friends who farm and ranch along the Milk River Valley, with whom I share a deep appreciation and affection for the prairie landscape.

To my best friend, Shirley Rose, and her two fine sons, John and Charlie, an affectionate thank-you for your friendship, warmth and good humour.

introduction

MOST PLACES HAVE a particular landscape feature which history and habit have made symbolic. The feature might be man-made, accepted over time as an integral part of the landscape — the San Francisco bridge or the white, high-steepled churches of Nova Scotia. Not so, however, in an area whose land forms tug at the very roots of the western plains heritage. Along the Montana/Alberta border, in the northwest corner of the Great Plains, the coulee stands out as a symbolic landform because it is not man-made. Rather, to the people of the high plains, its very wildness stands in affirmation of prairie culture.

Born in Montana, raised in Alberta, I was fortunate to grow up in the world of small prairie towns along the United States-Canadian border, almost equally at home in Shelby, Montana or Lethbridge, Alberta. It is a region where much has changed, both culturally and environmentally, since those youth filled years following World War II.

Accompanying the post-war urbanization of the West, there has been a shift in the connotation of the word 'coulee.' Like a trip to 'town,' 'coulee' meant much more than a place: it meant an entire community; the net sensation of a whole association of experiences, first-hand or rumoured, from the distant past, or the anticipated adventure tomorrow morning would bring.

In those days, cultural identity was determined by your role in the small town — a role which was, for the most part, predetermined by your parents' character and position, and subsequently tempered by your own choice of

figure 1: Coulee mouth, Milk River valley, Writing-On-Stone
Provincial Park

action and behavior. In contrast, out of town and away from the cultivated farmlands you entered the world of the prairie, the world of the coulee, from where there came an infinitely more acute sense of your own individuality, of your own presence.

In earlier years the feeling evoked by the word 'coulee' was one of natural presence, like something fresh and new, a biological culture unmarred, yet a place with history, rich with the mythical adventures of an earlier people. In a region where your own culture's presence began with your grandparents, to participate in the coulee's prairie community gave a sense of belonging which went beyond anything small town society could offer.

Today, the word 'coulee' evokes a somewhat different range of emotions. For the most part, that culturally reassuring sense of antithesis given by the prairie is gone. Today, like cultivated farmlands, most of the coulees are managed. Still, there are places . . . .

This little book is about the ecology of North American grasslands; it is about the relationships between the grassland organisms and their environments. More specifically, it is about the role of the coulee in the ecosystems of the northern plains including the landscapes of the southern portions of Manitoba, Saskatchewan and Alberta as well as much of Montana, Wyoming, North and South Dakota and Nebraska. It includes much of the great plains, roughly that area between the 98th meridian and the Rocky Mountains.

My own information comes primarily from the spectacular coulees adjacent to the Milk River valley and in the area of Writing-On-Stone Provincial Park (*figure 1*), Alberta. Unless otherwise noted, coulees referred to are from that region. In some cases the information relates specifically to the unique character of the Milk River region; less to coulees of other regions. Although the general relationships amongst the coulee creatures are relevant wherever coulees are found, the particular combinations of species and the inclusion of specific life history information here relates most directly to the coulees of southern Alberta. Particular reference to southeastern Alberta is made through much of the chapter on mammals. The author apologizes for the omission of many features unique to prairie coulees elsewhere. The hope remains that further attention will be given these fascinating and unique features of the prairie landscape.

To over-simplify a complex event is often misleading, whether in human events or in the study of natural history, but it is virtually impossible to describe and evaluate all of the interactions which contribute to the intricate workings of something as complex as an ecosystem. For practical purposes, this is a discussion of selected plants and animals, of bits and pieces of their life histories, combined with an introduction to the generalizations and principles by which ecologists order and comprehend their impressions of the natural world. It is an introduction to the natural history of coulees.

figure 2, opposite page: "V" shaped coulee, Pinhorn Grazing Reserve adjacent to the Milk River valley

the prairie and the coulee

FIFTY TO SEVENTY MILLION YEARS AGO, a region of the earth's crust near the western edge of North America ruptured, gradually thrusting skyward through the marine sediments of the Cretaceous to form the escarpments of the Rocky Mountains, a process geologists called the Laramide Revolution. The old beds of the Cretaceous seas became elevated to about five thousand feet above sea level. On the leeward eastern side of the newly formed mountains a rain shadow spread over the plains. The moisture-laden winds from the Pacific now dropped their water on the cool heights of the mountain slopes. Deprived of the rains which for millions of years had been carried eastward by the prevailing westerlies, the grasslands became dry and arid.

The formation of the rain shadow set the climatic stage for the grassland world which would follow. Erosion by ice and wind and water modified the eastward sloping plain. North of the 49th parallel, beginning about two million and ending about ten thousand years ago, the meltwater from the Pleistocene glaciation carved down the land — as much as two thousand feet in places — massively disrupting drainage patterns and topography. The glaciers deposited large amounts of debris carried as moraines, material from both east and west of the prairie flatlands: granite boulders from what are now Manitoba and Ontario, and quartzites from the western mountains. Proglacial streams, streams draining the meltwater lakes fronting the Pleistocene ice masses, carved great valleys. Today, the Milk, Oldman, South Saskatchewan and Red Deer rivers all run in post-glacial valleys. In southern Alberta, large coulees like Verdigris (*plate 1*), Etzikom, Chin and Pakowki, are all former glacial spillways.

The massive effects of glaciation dominate the surface topography of the plains north of the 49th parallel. The effects of glaciation diminish southward, but both north and south of the 49th parallel, water and wind erosion dispersed the rubble of ocean floor, disrupted and elevated by the processes of mountain formation. The elevated rock was worn bare, the eroded covering carried eastward onto the plains. By infinitesimal stages, the badlands and hills, coulees and ponds, lakes and streams formed the topography we associate with the prairies today.

Before the eruption of human technology and population, approximately one-quarter of the earth's land surface was covered with grass. In North America, Europe, Asia, on the African veldt and the Argentine pampas, the breeze passed with a freedom only unobstructed space could allow. As grassland ecosystems they were similar in many ways. Intimately personified by individuals and cultures of varying heritage and education, each grassland was unique.

On the prairie, in a landscape that seems, at first, to consist only of shimmering earth and pillow-clouded sky, there is a special diversity of environments. The most distinctive of these are the coulees.

As defined by Webster, a coulee is: "(a) small often intermittent stream, a dry creek bed sometimes running in a wet season, (b) a steep-walled valley or ravine varying widely in size and often having a stream at the bottom or (c) a small valley or low-lying area." The dictionary, however, cannot define the role of the coulee within the prairie biome. Among the native plant and animal communities of the flat North American steppes, the coulee is a unique variant. Although the original expanse of wilderness no longer exists on the western plains, it is within the coulees that we find the finest remnants of the great grassland ecosystem. Coulees, and the forested river bottoms which are sometimes nearby, at their best form natural wildland corridors of slightly modified grassland ecosystems, hemmed in by the biological desert of cultivated land (*plate 2*).

The name "coulee" was first used by early French Canadian voyageurs crossing the Great Plains. In their westward searches, they found the main water courses in a large area fringed with intricate systems of treeless valleys which they called coulees, from the French "couler," to flow. Some of these coulees had intermittent streams during the wet season, but most did not, and they varied from gentle depressions to steep-walled valleys or ravines.

To later residents of these large areas, especially those living in the northwestern portions — Alberta, Saskatchewan, and the adjoining states south — the word has become an essential component of everyday speech. When "hill" is up, "coulee" is down, the two words describing the principal landscape features in the grassy world of the prairie dweller.

Set within the original grasslands, coulees must have been traversed frequently by animals no longer present. It is exciting to imagine large herds of buffalo descending through coulees on their way to drinking water in late summer, or perhaps sheltering below during winter blizzards. But as man plowed ever more acres of arable land, and erected ever more fences, the coulees became increasingly isolated from their surroundings until they now appear to us, at least from the air, as many-fringed intrusions into the regular, controlled world of the cultivated prairie.

An ecosystem may be described as the system resulting from all of the interactions of the plant and animal communities functioning together with the non-living environment. In the existing agro-ecosystem of western Canada and the United States, domesticated plants, animals, and human communities proper contribute the largest portion of the biomass, the total mass of living organisms (*plate 3*). In the modern prairie ecosystem, which must include the domestic as well as the wild, probably the most appropriate concept of the coulee is as a reservoir of native plant and animal stocks, a variety of life forms complimentary to the flatland's cultivated monoculture.

As a landscape feature similar to the African "wadi" or the "arroyo" of the southwestern United States, a coulee is defined as a short, often straight, narrow, comparatively steep valley tributary to a perennial stream. Its normal direction follows that of the most direct drainage line resulting from runoff following the line of least resistance down the walls of the adjacent river valley. For example, several unusual and extensive series of coulees have developed along the Oldman River near Lethbridge. These run closely parallel to one another, apparently a consequence of the initial erosion by rain or snow being driven by the prevailing "chinook" winds of the area (Beaty, 1975a).

Like most stream-carved valleys, coulees are typically "V" shaped in cross section (*figure 2, p. 17*), the youngest, most recently developed possessing comparatively straight side slopes. Suggested average coulee dimensions are 100 to 500 metres in length by 50 to 200 metres in width and 50 to 80 metres in depth at the mouth (Beaty, 1975b). However, there are many exceptions. In the Writing-On-Stone Provincial Park area for example, as well as in the badlands adjacent to the large valleys of the South Saskatchewan, Red Deer and Milk Rivers, coulees running several miles and of several hundred feet in maximum depth are not uncommon. The typical "V" shape of these older coulees has been much modified by slumping and in some, particularly the spectacular sandstone walled coulees in and near Writing-On-Stone, by differential wind erosion of the coulee slopes (*plates 4 and 5*).

The floor of the average coulee tends to be flat and smooth, varying in width from one metre to as much as ten to twelve metres. In some areas, the name coulee is also applied to the large dry valleys, perhaps a kilometre in width, of prehistoric drainage channels. Although the rule is that coulees are generally dry valleys carrying runoff only after heavy rains or during snow melt, a few bear on their floors the relatively lush vegetation and greater number of habitants sustained by spring-fed streams. Realizing that the variety of life within the coulees provides the necessary balance for the continued functioning of the entire ecosystem, these coulees with permanent streams are of very special concern.

The greater the genetic diversity of a community, the healthier it is. In a biological community, most species are usually represented by moderate or few numbers. Only a few species have large numbers of individuals.

This pattern of a few common species associated with many less abundant forms is especially evident on the plains of Alberta where the many uncommon species tend to be concentrated within the diverse habitats of the coulees, while the few ecological dominants monopolize the flatlands above.

Contributing to species diversity is the coulee's role as ecotone. An ecotone is a region of transition or "tension" between two or more diverse communities; a conceptually "grey" zone which may be quite long but is narrower than the larger adjoining communities. One of the characteristics of an ecotone is the phenomenon known as "edge effect," resulting from the area's having a larger number of species, or greater species diversity, than the adjacent communities. Because it is a region of overlap, an ecotone possesses many organisms typical of the larger bordering communities plus organisms which are characteristic of and restricted to the ecotone proper.

To the ecologist, the ecotone is in itself an integrated ecosystem which may be conceptually isolated from the surrounding biome. In contrast, the biogeographer views the ecotone as a part of the environmental whole. The biogeographer might, for example, regard a coulee and river valley system such as that found in southern Alberta as a highway which permits the dispersal of woodland species into the normally unsuitable plains region, thereby allowing new and stable populations to become established in areas far from their historical ranges.

Cottontail rabbits, yellow-bellied marmots, raccoons, a subspecies of porcupine, the western silvery minnow and many others have spread along the wooded and wet valley bottoms, following the coulees northward into the shortgrass plains of Canada.

the gift of
water

To UNDERSTAND THE NATURE of a prairie stream, it has been suggested that one should follow it from its beginning as a small headwater, watching its changing environments as it joins other streams to form a river, and other rivers to form the great ocean-bound drainages of the continent. The origin of a prairie stream is not always obvious; there may be a slight difference in the way the grass lies, a more luxuriant growth, or perhaps small channels among the grasses as rain or snow melt seeps to lower ground. But, ultimately, the soil becomes saturated; it will hold no more, and water begins to move on water. As channels join, the creek bed becomes wider and more pronounced. The soils are worn away and hard gravel is sorted to form a bed. Occasionally a spring is uncovered from its subsurface existence, permitting the stream to run year-round (Costello, 1969) (*plate 6*).

At the water's edge, the wind-borne seeds of willows are among the first to become established. In turn, alders and cottonwoods send their roots into the soil, binding and strengthening the banks of the stream. Their shade permits snowberry (*plate 7*) and other shrubs to grow. In the flat alkali bottom of a coulee, a pond might be formed with bulrushes, reeds and cattails.

Of the diverse environments found within a coulee, none surpasses the tremendous variety of plants and animals which become linked together in aquatic food chains. In coulees with permanently flowing streams, the subsequent union of such chains with terrestrial patterns produces a biotic community of tremendous complexity.

The variety of aquatic life varies directly with the range of aquatic habitats. These, in turn, are dependent upon the degree of topographic diversity. Current, depth, water chemistry, bottom materials, temperature and erosional susceptibility are all abiotic factors affecting the composition of aquatic communities. Each combination of factors will produce a unique environment in which water-dwelling plants, animals, bacteria and fungi will interact to form a complex unique to each body of water. No two bodies of water nor even areas of the same pond or stream will possess the same flora and fauna.

Dependent upon features of topography, climate and soil, the character of aquatic habitats found within a coulee vary from deep pools with little aquatic vegetation to shallow, bottom-rich ponds and clear-flowing streams.

Prairie streams typically exhibit great seasonal fluctuations in flow. The greatest volume accompanies spring runoff; the lowest, termed the minimal volume, occurs during the frozen winter months and determines the basic productive capacity of a stream. If two streams are compared, other factors being equal, the one with the greatest stable flow will have the highest productivity. Under similar conditions of topography and climate, a stream with a constant source such as a lake or steadily flowing spring will be richer in aquatic organisms than another whose flow is sporadic and dependent on precipitation.

Bottom materials and temperature also affect productivity. In the grassland belt which parallels the Rocky Mountain wall, coulee streams flowing gently over the rich sods of the more eastern regions will be more productive than cooler, hard-bottomed streams of the foothill coulees to the west.

Most aquatic habitats can be classified on the basis of flowing (lentic) or non-flowing (lotic) water. Among the last are the pools and sloughs of the coulee bottom, usually shallow with fertile bottoms, rich in organic material and supporting lush communities of aquatic organisms.

Such ponds are ideal for many forms of aquatic plants and invertebrates. Pond algae like the slippery, bright green *Spirogyra*, rough-to-the-touch *Cladophora* and the green-brown grape-sized spheres of *Nostoc* at times form blooms which may briefly alter the appearance of the entire pond. Snails, various crustaceans, and seed shrimp thrive, transported from pond to pond via the feet of shorebirds or after passing unharmed through the digestive tracts of killdeer or mallard ducks. Shorebirds, feeding in water containing an abundant growth of aquatic plants are probably important dispersal agents for these small organisms.

Higher up the food chain, vertebrate populations of amphibians, reptiles, fish, birds and mammals are supported by the large numbers of aquatic plants and invertebrates of the coulee ponds. Frogs, salamanders and garter snakes as well as numerous species of shorebirds and prairie ducks are familiar residents of the coulee ponds. Mammals like muskrats, beaver and even the occasional mink may make their homes in or near the waters of the coulee bottoms (*plate 8*).

In contrast to the ponds and sloughs, the flowing waters of many coulees support abundant fish populations but provide fewer areas suitable for waterfowl or aquatic mammals. Usually, the rivers and coulee streams of the prairie maintain high oxygen levels and consistent top to bottom temperatures. Only those species adapted to the movement of flowing water can survive there. Iowa darters, fathead minnows, creek chub, common and mountain suckers, longnose dace and even the larger flathead chub, northern pike, and sauger may number among the fish of the West's coulee streams. The actual species composition depends upon the distance from the coulee mouth and the range of conditions prevailing within the tributary.

plants
the colour of a coulee

For PRACTICAL PURPOSES, the ecosystem is the basic functional unit of ecological study. It includes biotic communities and organisms as well as the abiotic or non-living environment. Because it emphasizes the fact that diverse organisms usually live together in an orderly manner, the concept of the "biotic community" is tremendously important to the ideas and principles of ecology.

Defined as any assemblage of populations living in a prescribed area or physical habitat, "biotic community" is a broad term, designating natural plant and animal groupings of various sizes. It is a living subdivision of the ecosystem, functioning as a unit through food chains and possessing characteristics additional to its individual and population components. In other words, the whole of a biotic community is greater than the sum of its parts.

This idea, of the unity of organisms and environment, seems difficult for many to understand: the comprehensive yet so simple concept that nature at any level is a perceived group of integrated phenomena, functioning together with "lower," "higher" and "equivalent" levels or strata, but always as part of a single integrated "whole." No organism can exist by itself or without an environment.

In the dry rain shadow of the Rockies, climatic conditions long ago determined the dominance of a drought-resistant flora tolerant of both arid conditions and saline soils. It is a land of harsh, unpredictable winters, hot summer winds and a high evaporation rate.

The prairie of much of Alberta and Montana is part of the semi-arid grass country of the high plains (*figure 3*), part of the earth's temperate grassland biome. Its climax vegetation is grass, though the dominant species may vary from region to region. Tall grass, mixed grass and shortgrass

figure 3, previous page: Vegetation detail, west rim of Verdigris coulee near its confluence with the Milk River — A typical shortgrass area with cacti, several types of sage and numerous other prairie forbs mixed with buffalo grass and blue grama.

prairies, the three major grassland zones into which the north temperate grasslands are divided, are all represented. Most abundant in the shortgrass regions are the sod-forming buffalo grass, introduced bluegrass, and blue grama. In the areas of mixed prairie, little bluestem, June grass, northern wheat grass and the speargrasses are more abundant.

Associated with each zone and found wherever local soil conditions permit, usually along roadsides or where overgrazing or the normal forces of erosion have removed the dominant grass growth, are the numerous non-grassy forbs (*plate 11*). Deep-rooted and broad-leaved, they are the prairie's flowering herbs and shrubs. Along roadsides, buffalo beans (golden bean, *Thermopsis rhombifolia*) and scarlet mallow are everywhere. Flixweed, common pepper grass, and loco-weed are common. Russian thistles grow wherever disturbance bares the prairie sod, their skeletons piling up in deep layers along fences and shelter belts and against the scattered growths of coulee brush.

In the shortgrass zone which dominates the more dramatic coulee and badland regions, sagebrush habitat covers large areas. Prickly pear and cushion cactus (*plates 9, 10, 12*), greasewood, salt sage (which is not a sage at all but a member of the Goosefoot family, also known as Nuttall's atriplex), sagebrush and winter fat are among the most common species. Yucca or soapweed (*plate 13*), common in Montana and south but in Alberta found only at a few localities along the Milk River, is one of the most interesting plants of the region. Not only is it an obvious example of a typically southern plains species whose northern range limits place it in an ecotonal zone among species more representative of northern communities, it is also a member of an insect-plant relationship in which growth and survival of both species is benefited. Neither can survive under natural conditions without the other.

The yucca plant reproduces only after fertilization by pollen transported by a specific type of moth. In turn, the young of the moth are specialized to the extent that only the yucca plant can provide them with food. In the evening, when the buds of the yucca open, the female *Pronuba* moth gathers pollen from the small anthers inside the flowers, rolling the sticky pollen into a tight little ball which is grasped by specialized mouthparts of the insect. The moth then flies to another flower, pierces the wall of the plant ovary with its ovipositor and deposits a batch of eggs among the young ovules. It then very deliberately proceeds to push its ball of pollen between the stigma lobes of the yucca, thus insuring fertilization of the plant. Upon hatching a few days later, the moth larvae feed on the developing seeds, utilizing about 20 per cent of the fertilized seeds in return for the pollination service. The larvae remain there until they are fully developed, whereupon they chew through the ovary wall, descend to the ground and pupate until the yucca again blossoms — when the pupae emerge as adult moths.

Within the grasslands, coulees provide habitats for a great diversity of plant types. In addition to the many species of forbs and sub-dominant grasses in the successive stages leading to development of the prairie's climax cover, other plants more typical of forested regions may also be present.

Within each coulee, plant distribution depends primarily on slope direction. The composition of the cover differs greatly on opposite sides of the coulee. This is especially evident in coulees which run approximately east-west. Because of their greater exposure to sunlight and the predominant west-southwest winds, south-facing slopes are warmer and drier than north-facing slopes. South-facing slopes are typically barren, supporting only sparse, drought-resistant plants. In contrast, protected from direct wind abuse and retaining the moisture of accumulated drifts of winter snows below their rims, the shaded north-facing slopes support a far greater plant cover.

On the exposed rims of some coulees, creeping juniper

forms thick carpets in the low shelter between rocks. Silver-berry or wolf willow forms dense, almost impenetrable growths. Moss phlox creeps into the smaller spaces and orange and green lichens (*plate 15*) cover the lee surfaces of rocks and boulders. Yellow bells (*plate 14*), shooting stars, low larkspur and many others may dot both the slopes and bottoms of the grassland valleys. In the sheltered coulee bottoms, bladder fern and red osier dogwood may be present, the last often forming dense canopies where moisture permits. Along the larger water courses occur a variety of willows, perhaps including the large peach-leaved willow and the smaller diamond willows. Where there are cottonwoods (*figure 4, p.32*), a dense thorny understory of wild rose, snowberry or buck brush, golden currant, chokecherry and thorny buffaloberry (*plate 16*) may form. River or black birch and western clematis occur, the first along permanent sheltered ponds bordered by horsetail and mossy patches covered with silverweed (*plate 18*). Groves of saskatoon grow on the upper slopes. Western Canada, yellow prairie and early blue violets (*plate 17*) occasionally make the coulee bottoms resemble more an eastern woodlot than what would be expected in a dryland coulee.

Each coulee is different. Its physiognomy and general appearance, its variety of diverse plant associations and species mixtures, are largely created by the different combinations of grasses, forbs, and shrubs, by the influence of the animals that live there and by topographic irregularities and a range of soil factors. Water supply, erosion and micro-climate vary from one coulee to the next. The combinations of forbs are never the same, from place to place, between seasons, and from year to year. Influenced by permutations of weather, grazing, and plant competition, by seed abundance and the unpredictability of seed dispersal by fruit-eating birds and mammals, each year the appearance of a coulee passes through a unique sequence of color and arrangement.

figure 4: Western cottonwood (*Populus sargentii*) — Although more typical of the specialized flora of the permanent prairie rivers, cottonwoods along with balsam poplar, Balm-of-Gilead, occasionally black poplar and others are found in the larger coulees, usually those with year-round water supplies.

The distinguishing plants of shortgrass prairie are the sod-forming blue grama and buffalo grasses. Beneath these grasses, the soil is characterized by a rich humus, formed from the decomposition of countless roots. Typically, it reaches down to the lime layer, a light-colored stratum of soil rich in minerals, primarily carbonates of calcium and magnesium, which marks the level to which rain water, and plant roots, penetrate (Allen, 1967). The depth of the layer depends on the yearly amount of precipitation. Where precipitation is low, below about fifty centimetres, this layer of alkali lies close to the surface. East and north, as precipitation increases, the lime layer will be progressively deeper until, where rain water is sufficient to reach down to subsoils permanently moistened by underground water, it disappears.

It has been estimated that in the form of roots — living and decaying — there is more organic material within the prairie soil than above it. From the abundantly branched, often fibrous roots of grasses, "a square yard of soil four inches deep may contain roots that would stretch for twenty miles if all were placed end to end" (Costello, p. 63). Among these roots and in the stems above lives a menagerie of smaller organisms. Crickets, ants, spiders, root-eating grubs, ground-dwelling bees and solitary wasps, an endless number of invertebrates, all live between, within, and below this strange diminutive jungle. Incredible numbers of micro-organisms exist there, an estimated "641,000 fungi and more than twenty million bacteria per gram of soil" (Costello, p. 78), decomposer organisms living on the dead remains of plants and animals. Without them, the total prairie ecosystem would quickly cease functioning. Neither the prairie and its plants, nor its birds, mammals or insects could exist without the tiny grassland fungi and bacteria.

birds

figure 5: Black-billed magpies (*Pica pica*)

The sharp-tailed grouse (*plate 20*), often wrongly called a prairie chicken, needs both brush and clearing. Caragana shelter belts, the patches of wild rose and buck brush on the open prairie and the woodlands and buffaloberry thickets of coulee bottoms are used by the grouse for shelter. Feeding on adjacent prairies or grain fields, the sharp-tail is a bird of brushy edges.

In late March or early April, between the last dirt-crusted drifts of winter snow, the males begin to gather on their ancestral dancing grounds. Arriving each morning and evening, in increasing numbers as the season advances, each male establishes his courting territory and performs his ritualized hen-attracting display.

In a photographer's blind set on the edge of a dancing-ground or "lek," there is little to be seen through the tiny peep holes to the outside world. In the dim light of dawn's first precious moments, the slightly ominous silhouette of a bison rubbing rock materializes and, to the northeast, the twinkling yard light of a distant ranch house.

A deep pulsing sound fills the air beyond the four foot cubicle of the blind. Soon, the already worn and trampled bit of prairie before the hide begins to fill with birds. In the half light, buffy gray shadows begin their border patrols. The crimson combs and bright purple of inflated neck sacs are still indistinct. Pattering their feet in a staccato crescendo, tail fans pointing slightly forward over their backs, more strutting males begin their territorial "dances." Border disputes erupt, sometimes ending in outright, wing-beating battles, more often culminating in a face-to-face, squatted stalemate until it is time to dance again.

By six or six-thirty, their colors are distinct. A little later the direct rays of the sun will wash them out again, all but orange and purple of comb and air sac. By then the males will be spread over the lek, on larger grounds perhaps over a couple of acres. Each guarded territory is bounded by imaginary lines which no other male may cross. Females wander disrespectfully from territory to territory but, finally, each will mate.

Later in the season, as the days lengthen, the level of activity diminishes. By mid-June the lek will be empty, the females dispersed to hatch their ten to fifteen olive-brown eggs in well hidden grass-lined hollows, the males to spend the summer in unconcerned, day-to-day routine.

Moving freely from coulee to shelter belt to open prairie, the sharp-tail grouse is a typical permeant, that is, an animal which "links" or couples biologically diverse communities and ecological subsystems. Moving freely amongst the various vegetation types of the prairie mosaic, permeants are highly mobile animals capable of exploiting the best of several worlds. Although migratory birds are the most spectacular permeants, the ecological role is one filled, to some degree, by almost all birds, mammals, and flying insects. Often, permeant "life histories are organized so that one stage is spent in one stratum or community and another stage in an entirely different stratum or community" (Odum, p. 377) under entirely different conditions.

Filling the ecological roles of insect eater, scavenger, predator and permeant, perhaps the most typical of all coulee birds is the black-billed magpie (*figure 5, p.36*). Its nests are common in any wooded coulee: over-sized creations consisting of an inner cup the size of a pigeon nest of mud or manure, plant fibers and small twigs, surrounded by a protective tangle one half to two metres long and a quarter to half a metre in diameter, made of woven sticks. Because of the magpie's long tail, the covered nest usually has two openings. The nests are usually built in tall trees or thorny shrubs but, unfortunately for humans, farm buildings and telephone wires also make suitable sites.

The magpie is one of the most controversial birds of the prairie. Guilty of depredations from nest robbing to stealing young chickens, and persistently enlarging the lesions started by warble fly larvae in the backs of livestock, this intelligent year-round resident will, on occasion, make a tremendous nuisance of itself. On the other hand, still in economic terms, its role as insectivore and scavenger makes the magpie indispensable, especially in clearing the grassland of carrion.

Equally controversial for their predations are the prairie birds of prey: the eagles, falcons, hawks and owls. Golden eagles (*plate 19*), ferruginous and Swainson hawks, prairie falcons (*plate 21*) and kestrels (sparrow hawks) and great horned and short-eared owls (*plates 22, 23*) are all hunters of the coulees.

The most characteristic of coulee raptors are the big broad-winged soaring hawks, the buteos or buzzard hawks which feed on small mammals such as mice, ground squirrels, rabbits and marmots. The nests of the fringe-legged ferruginous hawks (*figure 6*) are the most conspicuous in the border country coulees. Circling in big lazy circles high overhead or standing sentinel-like on telephone poles

figure 6: Young ferruginous hawks (*Buteo regalis*)

or hilltops, the adult ferruginous hawk is one of the largest birds of prey occurring in the grasslands. With a wingspan of about 140 cm and a total length of 60 to 65 cm, the "gopher hawk" is smaller than only the golden and bald eagles and the much rarer turkey vulture.

Returning north from Mexico in notably large spring flocks, the smaller Swainson hawk is the most abundant buteo of the shortgrass plains. It is distinguished by a dark russet collar or breast band, slate grey, hood-like head covering and pointed wings. Unlike the ferruginous hawk, its tree-nesting and insect eating habits (especially grass-hoppers) cause it to frequent shelter belts and the high grasslands more often than the coulees. In times of abundance, however, it will nest wherever suitable sites exist, frequently within coulees.

To many, the return of the migratory birds during the transitional green-up period between late winter and mid-spring represents the "re-birth" of spring. For a period of several weeks each spring, the coulees and grasslands come alive with the northward moving birds, each one with its own intense purpose. The meadowlark's royal melodies pronounce the new kingdom each individual has claimed, as do the frequent jinglings of male horned larks, singing out in flight high over the grass, warning other males against invading this patch of prairie.

Avocets, marbled godwits and willets have returned to build their nests edging the water holes; red-winged and yellow-headed blackbirds (*plate 24*) to build theirs in the tall reeds and cattails around the sloughs of the coulee bottom. The largest native shorebird, the long-billed cur-lew with its 20 cm, downward-curving bill has returned, as has the raucous killdeer. Both curlew and killdeer nest away from the water, a kilometre and a half or more. Both have long, pointed wings and a swift, graceful flight and their courtships involve elaborate aerial acrobatics and brilliant terrestrial displays of plumage. In both species, males and females cooperate to raise the young. Both killdeer and curlews, like many of the larger ground nesting birds, have shrill, far-reaching calls and perform elaborate broken wing routines to draw intruders away from their nests.

Usually, the greater the diversity of terrain, the greater is the variety of species occupying the ecosystem. An amazing range of habitats are available for birds on the prairie, the greatest concentration of which occur within the coulees. The "habitat" of an organism has been described as the address, the "niche" of an organism as its business or profession. The ecological niche of an organism depends not only on where it lives but also on what it does (how it transforms energy, behaves, responds to and modifies its physical and biotic environment), and how it is constrained by other species (Odum, 1971).

Within a coulee, each species has its own niche in the habitat it has selected. Herons, ducks, and geese; grebes, coots, rails, and sandpipers live about the ponds and streams of those coulee bottoms supplied with water. Prairie falcons, ferruginous hawks, sparrow hawks and swallows (*plate 27*) nest in the cliffs above and magpies, chickadees, juncos, and − in winter − rosy finches fill the woody thickets of bottom and slope. Wherever there is grass there are meadowlarks and longspurs, both chestnut-collared and McCown's; lark buntings, bobolinks, horned larks, and the myriad of sparrows often as not referred to, whether in desperation or resignation, as LGBs (little grey birds). Wherever there are holes and crevices in the baked clay of coulee banks, a rock wren might be found.

The avian fauna provide the most dramatic examples of the edge effect described earlier. An exceptional abundance and variety of species typify the coulees of southern Alberta. Along the edges of wooded thickets in the foothill coulees, male lazuli buntings space out their territories, frequently the brushy tangled thickets of saskatoon and chokecherry bordering the coulee sides. In drier coulees eastward, catbirds, brown thrashers, prairie warblers and song sparrows divide up the less available thicket-edge habitat in similar fashion. The niche of each is unique. Some move daily, even hourly, between prairie and coulee, between dry upland and coulee pond or from thicket to cliff. Others — the warblers, flycatchers and many sparrows — carry out their activities within the brushy tangles, rarely moving beyond the protective outer barrier of thorns, and then only to flick in quick silence to the next grove of thorny buffaloberry.

mammals

THE CLIFF IS QUIET, bathing in the first rosy hues of dawn. On a tiny patch of creeping juniper, the crystals of dew on a spider's forgotten lacework wear a silent sheen, not yet the twinkle that will startle the world with the sun's first direct rays. In a rising crescendo, tiny birds begin to announce the new and brighter hues rinsing the cliff. Two young ferruginous hawks start their morning preening in a nest strategically placed a few feet below the coulee's rim.

As the sun chips the edge of the eastern sky, a sudden silence deafens the land. Minutes pass. Then comes a sound, deep and barely audible, a low rumbling like muttering from the earth itself. As the calm before the storm, the silence fans beyond the growing din. Far to the south the sun's rays glow upon the heaviness of still wet morning air, filling with the dust raised by trampling hooves. Closer now, forms appear, the darkness of figures in flight; and others, upright and smaller on the margin of the mass, the pursuers. It is the day of the buffalo jump, the pishkun.

Opposite the cliff of the young hawks is another precipice, north-facing, still in shade. The herd is close now. Pressed by the terrible momentum of a hundred hurtling forms, the lead shape stumbles in a futile, desperate attempt to turn.

Below are the waiting boulders and the too-luxuriant green of grass growing in soil dark and rich with the accumulated bones of fifteen hundred years. There too, sixty feet below, are the waiting men.

Some five hundred years ago, it is probable that the undeveloped North American grasslands supported between fifty and seventy million bison (*plate 25*), living in grazing bands of fifty to two hundred animals. Adult males weigh 800 to 1000 kilograms, females 400 to 500 kilograms; obviously, humans living in the midst of such an immense biomass would make abundant use of it. It has been estimated that the Blackfoot made more than eighty separate items from the carcasses of bison; from hide tipi coverings to clothing, meat and a wide variety of horn and bone implements (*plate 26*).

Discussing the decimation of the bison herds, Durward L. Allen wrote, "The final arbiter of [the buffalo's] destiny was the fertility of his native range. He had to pass because of changed conditions. And yet we know that the great herds would have been wiped out whether or not plow ever broke the prairie sod. The killing was calculated." In a biography of Kootenai Brown, southern Alberta's best known frontiersman and the first superintendent of Waterton Lakes National Park, author William Rodney discusses a quotation of Brown's. "There were countless thousands of buffalo in those days, thicker than even range cattle on any range on earth. I have stood on the top of the Cypress and Sweet Grass Hills in Alberta and Saskatchewan and as far as I could see in all directions was a living mass of buffalo. . . ." Rodney adds, "By 1878 . . . there were no buffalo in the Cypress Hills, and none between the Milk River and the Missouri, the area in which Kootenai hunted." (Rodney, 1969).

Before European settlement, the great bison herds dominated the prairie grasslands, perhaps, like cattle today, finding refuge from winter storms within the sheltering coulees. With their head and shoulders heavily protected by a warm coat of wool, bison were well prepared to face the blizzards of the northern plains. However, through the long months of winter, to animals weakened by hunger and cold, even the smallest advantage could make the difference between death and survival.

It is unlikely that we will ever be certain what parts the large free-roaming herds of bison and antelope played within the ecosystem of the prairie valleys. Like other dominant creatures of the early prairie — the plains grizzly, the wolf, the early human hunters — the great grassland herds were all part of a prairie world we can now only imagine, an unending play from which the first acts are missing. As in a play, each grassland scene has its own special façade, each act its own cast, acting out their lives on a stage set by wind and rain and sun.

If one examines a map of the major life regions of North America, it soon becomes obvious that temperature and humidity, and climatic conditions in general, play the dominant role in determining the vegetation type of a region, whether desert, semi-arid grassland or humid to wet forest. In turn, the vegetation type of a particular area largely determines the animals that may survive there. In southeastern Alberta, the combination of the lowest precipitation with the highest temperatures makes this portion of North America's third prairie steppe the most arid part of Canada's high plains. Referred to variously as "arid," "semi-arid" or "mid-latitude steppe," the climate of the southeastern coulees and adjacent prairies is reflected in its wildlife in such features as coloration, timing of individual behavior patterns and, at the highest level of organization, the actual species composition of the plain's ecosystem.

One hundred and fifty-three distinct forms of mammals, either species or subspecies, occur within the province of Alberta (Soper, 1964). More than fifty-eight of these have been recorded from the southeastern quarter of the province.

Among the mammals of the coulee, shrews, for their size, are undoubtedly the most aggressive animals of the prairie. Though they are primarily insectivorous, neither of the two species occurring in southern Alberta will hesitate to attack rodents much larger than themselves. Smaller even than the prairie dusky shrew, the cinereous shrew is one of the smallest of Alberta's mammals, with an average adult weight of 3.7 grams.

Of the secretive nocturnal mammals of the prairie, bats are the least known. In late summer evenings, just before dark, they may appear as dark, flitting silhouettes against the not-as-dark, blue-black patches of sky spanning the tops of coulee-bottom cottonwoods.

Six species of bats occur within Alberta. Of these, the

pale big-eared and the Say masked bat are habitual summer residents of the southern part of the province. In western Canada as a whole, the pale big-eared bat can be considered to occur only as a straggler. Like the red bat, whose occasional presence is considered accidental, it is typically a more southern species.

Most bats migrate south, though a few will hibernate, roosting in clusters or singly in trees, crevices in the sandstone cliffs of suitable coulees, or in abandoned buildings. The silver-haired and hoary bats which frequent Alberta's northern wooded areas appear in the southern part of Alberta during their migrations to and from the subtropics.

Neither the little brown nor the big brown bat is known to migrate in any numbers. Occurring throughout Alberta and Saskatchewan, they are, in order, the two most common bats of the area.

The jackrabbit or white-tailed prairie hare (*plate 28*) is built for survival by flight. Its sharp eyes and large, sensitive ears efficiently warn of danger and its strong hind legs enable it to cross the prairie at speeds reported up to seventy kilometres an hour, with single leaps reaching more than six and a half metres.

Prey for a large number of predators, jackrabbits flourish throughout the prairies, relying for survival on a high birth rate and large numbers of individuals. Their numbers fluctuate between periods of abundance and scarcity, at times increasing locally to plague proportions. Though frequently found within the coulees, the jackrabbit, like the pronghorn, is better suited to the open plains. It is adapted for looking, listening and running; in short, for survival in the open. Both of these plains runners use only shallow depressions or "forms" when resting, shallow beds perhaps slightly excavated and situated to the greatest visual advantage.

Like the jackrabbit, numbers of the related varying hare (snowshoe rabbit) fluctuate widely. Its numbers originally noted in fur records of the Hudson Bay Company, its cyclic abundance and scarcity are well known, as is the attendant population cycle of its chief predator, the Canada lynx. The average time between peaks of the snowshoe rabbit cycle is 9.6 years. Within the area, snowshoe rabbits occur in varying densities within the wooded foothill coulees along the western edge of the region, and an isolated population is found in the mixed forest of the Cypress Hills.

The third member of the rabbit family found in southeastern Alberta is the Black Hills race of the cottontail rabbit (*plate 29*). Common throughout the United States, in Alberta, the species is at the northern end of its range. Sparsely distributed, it is found only in the southern part of the province, north to about Red Deer.

Coulees and river valleys provide most of the cottontail's habitat in Alberta. To survive in an area, the species must have adequate cover for escape, especially in winter when woody forbs provide both food and protection from predators and climatic elements. In warmer latitudes south of Alberta, female cottontails may have as many as five litters each year. Housing four to seven blind, hairless young, the nest, often hidden beneath rock and boulder-strewn coulee outcrops, is lined with dry grass and tufts of the doe's fur. Within two weeks of birth the young are moving from the nest. Some will breed and raise their own litters this first summer but most will bear their first litters the following spring.

The order Rodentia (rodents), containing many of the most interesting and attractive forms of mammals, is represented in southern Alberta by twenty-three species, almost one-half of the mammalian forms found in the southeast corner of the Province.

Not definitely recorded in Alberta before 1952, yellow-bellied marmots (*plate 30*) have appeared only recently in the valley and adjoining coulees of the Milk River. It has been suggested that the species probably emigrated from

plate 1, top: Verdigris coulee — Like many of southern Alberta's larger coulees and river valleys, Verdigris is a proglacial river valley: a valley carved by streams draining the large lakes found along the southern borders of thawing Pleistocene glaciers.

plate 2, bottom: Stubble fields, southern Alberta — On the western plains of Canada and the Northwestern United States, almost all arable lands have been cultivated; in its original sense, wilderness, the "place of the wild beast," no longer exists. Today, coulees are the prairie's wilderness.

plate 3, top: Cattle drive, Van Cleeve coulee — Often providing the only available shelter from winter storms and summer heat, coulees are much more than just recreationally and aesthetically important. Their vegetation and water resources are essential to the economy of many prairie ranches. Unfortunately, overgrazing and other abuse deprives all of an irreplaceable resource.

plate 4, bottom: Police Coulee, Writing-On-Stone Provincial Park

plate 5, above: Van Cleeve coulee, west of Writing-On-Stone Provincial Park

plate 6, left: Spring runoff, Van Cleeve coulee — A spring-fed stream which normally flows through most of the summer months

51

from top to bottom:

plate 7: Snowberry (*Symphoricarpos albus*) — Characterized by its round waxy-white berries, snowberry is widely used for food by browsing ungulates like mule and white-tailed deer. It is better known in forest and parkland regions but is found in wooded coulees with good water supplies.

plate 8: Pintails (*Anas acuta*) — Of the many species of waterfowl found on prairie sloughs and ponds, both within the coulees and on the flatlands, pintails and mallards are the best known.

plate 9: Prickly pear cactus (*Opuntia polyacantha*)

plate 10: Cushion cactus (*Mamillaria vivipara*)

plate 11: Vegetation detail, coulee rim, southern Alberta — The three most prominent plants are pasture sage (*Artemisia frigida*), cushion cactus (*Mamillaria vivipara*) and yellow sweet clover (*Melilotus officinalis*), an introduced species.

plate 12, top: Greasewood
(*Sarcobatus vermiculatus*)

plate 13, middle: Spanish
bayonet or yucca (*Yucca glauca*)

plate 14, bottom: Yellow bell or
fritillaria (*Fritillaria pudica*) — A
tiny lily, not common, found
flowering early in the season on
a sheltered, east-facing slope.

54

from top to bottom:

plate 15: Lichens on boulder surface, Haffner coulee

plate 16: Thorns and blossoms, thorny buffaloberry (*Shepherdia argentea*) — A typical coulee shrub which may reach five metres in height, forming dense impenetrable thickets. Distinguished by its silvery leaves and branches and by its paired thorns.

plate 17: Early blue violet (*Viola adunca*) — Found only in the most secluded coulee glens, near springs or by a silent shaded bend of a coulee stream.

plate 18: Silverweed (*Potentilla anserina*) — A showy, yellow-flowered cinquefoil which grows in thick mats along the margins of sloughs or in low wet meadows.

plate 19, top: Golden eagle (*Aquila chrysaetos*) — Though usually too scarce to be considered a typical coulee dweller, when numbers are adequate the nests of golden eagles can be found either on inaccesible cliff faces or high atop a coulee-bottom poplar. Two such nests are known by the author in the Writing-On-Stone area.

plate 20, above left: Sharp-tailed grouse (*Pedioecetes phasianellus*) — Males displaying on their dancing ground or "lek."

plate 21, above right: Prairie falcon (*Falco mexicanus*)

from top to bottom:

plate 22: Young great horned owls (*Bubo virginianus*) — The young are hatched in the abandoned tree nests of Swainson's hawks and magpies, as well as in the tiny wind-hollowed caves of sandstone cliffs.

plate 23: Short-eared owl (*Asio flammeus*)

plate 24: Yellow-headed blackbird (*Xanthocephalus xanthocephalus*)

57

from top to bottom:

plate 25: Plains bison
(*Bison bison*)

plate 26: A "tipi ring"
on the edge of a coulee
near the Milk River
valley — Such rock
rings were probably
used to hold down the
outer edges of the
buffalo hide lodges
used by the plain's
Indians.

plate 27: Tree swallows
(*Iridoprocne bicolor*)

plate 28, top:
White-tailed
prairie hare or
white-tailed
jackrabbit (*Lepus
townsendii*)

plate 29, middle:
Black Hills
cottontail rabbit
(*Sylvilagus
nuttallii*)

plate 30, bottom:
Yellow-bellied
marmot (*Marmota
flaviventris*)

NATURAL UNIVERSITY. COLLEGE
LIBRARY

plate 31, top: Porcupine (*Erethizon dorsatum*)

plate 32, middle: Mule deer (*Odocoileus hemionus*)

plate 33, bottom: Fawn, white-tailed deer (*Odocoileus virginianus*) — The white spots, so typical of fawn coloration, resemble spots of sunlight on vegetation. The spots serve to disrupt the outline of the motionless young animals, thus protecting them from predators.

plate 34, top:
Red fox pups
(*Vulpes fulva*)

plate 35, middle:
Short-tailed weasel
(*Mustela erminea*)

plate 36, bottom:
Bobcat (*Lynx rufus*)

61

from top to bottom:

plate 37:
Ground blizzard, Milk
River valley

plate 38:
Yellow stoneseed
(*Lithospermum incisum*)

plate 39: Prairie
anemone or crocus
(*Anemone patens*)

plate 40, top:
Eastern short-
horned lizard
(*Phrynosoma
douglassi*)

plate 41, middle:
Grasshoppers on
abandoned grain
wagon

plate 42, bottom:
Prairie rattle-
snake den
(*Crotalus viridis*)

plate 43: Coulee bottom slough, mid-summer

the mountain region of western Montana and Idaho.

Ground squirrels, close relatives of the marmot, are among the best known of prairie mammals. Their life histories are particularly interesting, their ecological roles both essential and fascinating. Burrowing rodents, they readily appropriate the barren patches of soil revealed by overgrazing and erosion. Their tilling loosens, aerates and mixes the soil and, in turn, annual weedy forbs invade the sites of their disturbance, beginning the natural processes of revegetation.

Living primarily on the grains, tubers, fruits and leaves of vegetation, ground squirrels spend much of their active time putting up food stores to be used in early spring or during drought or other periods of food scarcity. As well as vegetable matter, their diet includes many forms of insects — grasshoppers, ants, beetles, crickets, even young mice — all taken as opportunity offers.

True hibernators, they need no food in winter; body fat acquired during the previous fall provides the minimum amount of energy needed until spring awakening. Ground squirrels usually hibernate from October to April. Curled up in a subterranean nest, the temperature of the animal drops and its pulse rate slows. It breathes only a few times a minute. In addition to winter hibernation, in some areas ground squirrels retreat underground again during the hot dry period of mid-summer; this dormant or inactive period induced by summer heat is referred to as aestivation.

Ground squirrels and many other rodents of the arid grasslands seldom, if ever, drink. By moving below ground during hot dry periods, loss of water by evaporation is minimized. In addition, their kidneys are built to recover the maximum amounts of water from urinary wastes. Some rodents, like the kangaroo rat, pass virtually no liquid wastes, the urine being reduced to crystals of uric acid to be removed by defecation. Necessary water is obtained from even very dry foods as a by-product of cellular metabolism. Products of digestion are circulated via the blood stream to the tissues, where individual cells absorb them for energy and growth in a metabolic process somewhat resembling internal combustion. During this process of chemical reaction, combining the digestive products with oxygen from the lungs, needed water is produced as a by-product.

Usually referred to erroneously as a "gopher," Richardson's ground squirrel (*figure 7*) is one of the prairie's most common mammals, certainly the most abundant ground squirrel. Living in loose colonies of underground tunnel complexes which may go down one and a half metres and be fifteen or more metres in length, their population densities may be in the hundreds per hectare in times of abundance. Relying less on the shelter of the coulees than on the protection of large numbers, protective coloration, and a workable alarm system of loud whistles and switching tails, they are well adapted for

figure 7: Richardson ground squirrels or "gophers" (*Spermophilus richardsonni*)

living on the open expanses of grassland, where their high-set eyes and low rounded heads let them view their surroundings while they themselves remain barely visible above the soil of their mounds.

More typical of the coulees is the thirteen-lined ground squirrel. Smaller, the size of a large chipmunk, it is conspicuously marked with alternating stripes of dark brown and buff, each light buff stripe broken into dots. The entrance holes to its burrows are hidden within the brush patches, unmarked by the dirt mounds so typical of the Richardson's ground squirrel. Its burrows are winding and shallow, six metre long trenches or tunnels with one chamber containing a thick nest of grasses, another a food store of miscellaneous plant parts, the excavated soil scattered and lost in the surrounding vegetation.

Lesser known and perhaps the most unusual of Alberta's prairie mammals is the Anderson race of the Richardson pocket gopher. As shown by examining a series of specimen skins obtained over the length of the province, Anderson's pocket gophers found in the south — like the beaver and the pallid vole — exhibit the pale coloration adaptive to the arid landscape. Nocturnal creatures, they rarely venture abroad in daylight. Like Richardson's ground squirrel, pocket gophers live in loose colonies evidenced by the fan-shaped mounds of loose earth with no visible opening, as though the soil had been pushed up from below. Though rarely seen, they are undoubtedly the grassland's finest excavators.

The pocket gopher is named for the two externally-opening, fur-lined cheek pockets in which it carries food or nesting material. For chewing the gritty bulbs and roots upon which it feeds, the pocket gopher's chisel-like incisor teeth are located in front of the lips. The lips fold in and meet behind the incisors, keeping dirt from entering the mouth while the animal chews. Like the beaver's, the front teeth of the pocket gopher grow continuously to compensate for their rapid wear. The lower pair may grow as much

figure 8: White-footed mouse (*Peromyscus maniculatus*)

as thirty-six centimetres in a year.

The burrows of one pocket gopher may be 150 metres in length and cover half a hectare of ground. Loosening the earth with its teeth and the heavy claws of its short, spade-like front feet, the muscular 450-gram gopher places its head and front feet against a plug of soil and bulldozes the load up and out a vertical shaft to its surface dump. Its fine, silky fur offers little resistance to its passage through the tunnel in either direction.

There are three species of white-footed mice found within the coulees of southeastern Alberta, all members of the genus *Peromyscus* (*figure 8*). The Osgood white-footed mouse is the most common small mammal of the area while its close relative, the badlands white-footed mouse is relatively scarce, apparently confined to the Milk River drainage.

Trim, white-bellied, brown-backed mice with large black

figure 9: Meadow vole (*Microtus pennsylvanicus*)

eyes and long, sensitive whiskers, the species of *Peromyscus*, like most small mice, are nocturnal, abroad only at night and living underground during the day. Their diet consists of seeds, small nuts and fruit pits, occasionally supplemented by insects or other meats when these are available. Their teeth, those in the cheek blunted with rounded tubercles designed for mashing up seeds, are indicative of their vegetarian diet.

Though it is usually not plentiful, the badlands meadow vole or "meadow mouse" occurs over the entire area (*figure 9*). It is a chunky, solid grey rodent with short legs and tail and small eyes, lacking the handsome delicacy of the deer mice. Also unlike the deer mice, meadow voles usually remain on well-trodden runways during their foragings. Wherever the animals occur there is a maze of tunnel-like paths among and through the ground-level vegetation. Like other mammalian grass-eaters, including such large forms as bison and cattle, the vole's cheek teeth have a flattened grinding surface, patterned with shearing triangles formed of sharp enamel ridges, very unlike the crushing tubercles of the deer mice.

The prairie harvest mouse, Audubon grasshopper mouse and the pallid vole are the three rarest mice in the area. The harvest mouse remained unnoticed in southeastern Alberta until 1951.

Named for its diet of grasshoppers and other insects, the grasshopper mouse is insectivorous, unusual among rodents. In true predator fashion, in addition to its typical mousy squeak it reportedly also has a shrill whistle, something of a lilliputian wolf howl.

Alberta's plains have still two more species of mice, both unusual. The average length of an adult Saskatchewan jumping mouse is a little under 23 cm; of that, 13 cm is tail. With its long tail and powerful back legs, it is a jumper, capable of 2.5 metre leaps. It is most common in areas of moist ground, usually in heavier upland prairies or along the wooded borders of streams. Like the species of *Peromyscus*, it is a seed eater. Protected by an insulating cover of snow, most mice are able to carry on with their normal daily activities throughout the winter months but, unlike Alberta's other native mice, the jumping mouse is a true hibernator.

Named for its fur-lined cheek pockets not unlike those of the pocket gopher, the Maximilian pocket mouse is probably Alberta's least known mammal. Like the jumping mouse, the pocket mouse travels like a diminutive kangaroo on its large hind legs, using its long tufted tail for balance.

The three remaining rodents occurring in Alberta's coulees are the porcupine, the muskrat and the beaver, the latter two limited by their aquatic natures to those coulees with permanent streams or sloughs.

The porcupine lives on a diet of grain or forage crops when these are available. Otherwise, it browses on the twigs and bark of willows and other shrubs and trees. The porcupine (*plate 31*), though more common in the wooded valleys, might be found trundling peacefully along a deer trail within even the most barren coulee.

The best known mammals of the coulees are those which man hunts, especially the larger forms: coyotes, bobcats and deer.

In most prairie coulees, where mule deer populations exist they, along with livestock, are the ecological dominants (*plate 32*). The mule deer is a twilight species of the forest's edge. In the southeastern plains, it spends most of its daylight time within the shelter of coulee brush patches. At evening and early morning it emerges from the protective cover to feed and water, its diet consisting primarily of the twigs, leaves and buds of shrubs and trees.

The antlers of the bucks begin to grow in spring. Growth continues until late summer or early fall when the "velvet," by which the enlarging beams are nourished, is shredded and discarded. On exposure, the antlers harden into the finished armament of the jousting male. Males are promiscuous or casual breeders: although they will join and accompany bands of females during the breeding season, they do not collect groups of does (harems) in the strict sense of polygamy. Neither do they participate in caring for the young.

Odorless and wearing the protectively-coloured "Bambi" coat, fawns are born in May after a 215 day gestation period (*plate 33*). Although the number of fawns per doe varies from one to three, twins are most common.

In summer, adult males remain apart from females and immatures. While the year's young remain with the adult female, older males seek more remote areas and the solitude of their own company, or perhaps the restricted companionship of a few other males.

The cooler temperatures of autumn release the hormonal flow which stimulates the reproductive urge or rut. The reddish summer coats of both does and bucks are replaced by the stone-grey winter pelage. The neck regions of the males begin to swell and they begin associating with the bands of does and fawns. As the breeding season approaches, males grow more restless and increasingly aggressive toward other bucks. After breeding the bucks lose their antlers, usually in January and February. As spring approaches, the large groups of winter once again begin to disperse, the females to give birth and the males to resume their solitary bachelorhood.

The mule deer has been the most common member of the cloven-hoofed mammals in this area for the past fifty years. Since settlement, its distribution has been reduced to relatively undisturbed areas, its survival in most regions wholly dependent on adequate game management programs. In contrast, the white-tailed deer is more adaptable. Though once scarce in the prairie provinces, its range is now increasing and it is quite common on the farm and ranchlands of southern Alberta. Though it intermittently utilizes the coulees for cover or winter sheltering areas, the life history of the white-tail is more appropriately associated with open farm and grasslands than with the coulee habitat proper.

Coyotes (*figure 10*) are introduced habitually with emotionally-based descriptions. Without doubt the image of the coyote is emotional, full of equal doses of admiration and contempt. Our mental images of the coyote do symbolize the coulees: they represent equally the romantic, historical aspects and the imaginative, recreational ones. Unfortunately, the coyote's biological role in the grassland ecosystem is still only poorly understood. The difficulty of working with wild populations of coyotes has allowed little more than speculation on the animal's cumulative effect on other wildlife.

Relatively small members of the dog family, adult male coyotes average 13.5 kg and adult females twelve. They stand about half a metre at the front shoulders. The popular concept of coyotes is that they are much larger;

however, in a survey within the state of Kansas, the weights of 300 coyotes ranged from 8 to 19.5 kg.

Courtship and mating usually take place in late January through February. Pairs remain together, often for several years, the male assuming the duties of a father in both caring directly for the young and at times hunting for food for the entire family.

The litter, usually five or six blind and helpless pups, is born in March or April after a gestation period of sixty to sixty-three days. The den, prepared by the female, is often an enlarged badger hole dug in a coulee slope, but where there is a shortage of preferred sites, a hollow tree, rock pile, or even the space beneath a granary may be used. The female may begin excavating several den sites before finally settling on one to use but even the most ideal will be quickly abandoned and the pups rapidly moved to a new

figure 10: Prairie coyote (*Canis latrans*)

location if the site is disturbed.

Rabbits, hares and rodents make up the bulk of coyotes' diet. Generally inactive from about one in the morning to daybreak and between mid-morning and late afternoon, most of their foraging takes place in the first few hours after dark. Coyotes are opportunists, taking whatever food is most easily obtained. Unfortunately, if the most available item happens to be an unprotected lamb or fawn, coyotes will take quick advantage of the situation, especially if the individual has had an earlier opportunity to practice and perfect the habit. It is a habit which has gotten the species into all kinds of trouble with its greatest competitor, man.

Of the large carnivores which frequented the coulees and plains before settlement, only coyotes, bobcats and red foxes (*plate 34*) remain. The wolves, swift foxes, black-footed ferrets and plains grizzlies were all exterminated. In *Lives of Game Animals*, Ernest Thompson Seton notes a specimen of the Great Plains wolf killed in North Dakota which weighed 168 pounds. Typically weighing well over one hundred pounds, such animals were the principal predator of the plains bison herds. Once plentiful in the Cypress Hills as well as on the adjacent plains among the bison and antelope herds, the last plains grizzlies of southeastern Alberta were probably those killed within the Cypress Hills in the late 1800s.

Easily trapped or poisoned, the small swift fox, about the size of a domestic cat and equally inquisitive, was last recorded in Alberta on May 3, 1938, east of Manyberries. Swift foxes have recently been re-introduced to southeastern Alberta and southwestern Saskatchewan; however, the success of their introduction is still uncertain.

The black-footed ferret, now the rarest North American member of the weasel family, disappeared from Canada almost without notice. A 1981 discovery of a population in northwest Wyoming has renewed hope for the species' survival. Today, the recovery of the black-footed ferret

figure 11: American badger (*Taxidea taxus*)

depends on the success of a small captive population being cared for in a breeding facility in Laramie, Wyoming. Wildlife departments in both the U.S and Canada have issued urgent requests that any sightings be reported as quickly as possible to a fish and wildlife officer.

Of the coulee's remaining carnivores, six are also members of the weasel family: the American badger (*figure 11*), the northern plains skunk, the Hudson Bay mink and the long-tailed, short-tailed and least weasels. Of the three weasels, all of which turn white in winter, the long-tailed is the most numerous in the south. The short-tailed weasel is more typically associated with parkland and forest (*plate 35*). Weighing only 55 to 85 grams, the rarely seen least weasel is considered to be the smallest living member of the order Carnivora.

Probably more abundant than realized, the ecological role of raccoons within Alberta is still uncertain. Their sign is common in many of the wooded coulee bottoms of the south, and increasing numbers of raccoons are appearing as road kills or as unwelcome midnight visitors to garden plots and chicken coops. Like the marmot, their immigration has been recent, probably north along the Milk River from Montana.

The cat family, Felidae, is represented by three native species of which only one is a typical coulee resident, the pallid barred bobcat (*plate 36*). Because of their secretive nature, bobcats are rarely seen. Feeding on cottontails, small rodents and the occasional grouse, their numbers are probably quite stable.

Neither the Canada lynx nor the Rocky Mountain cougar can be considered plains residents. Depending almost entirely on the varying hare for food, numbers of lynx will on occasion venture out onto the plains and coulees when their food supply suffers one of its periodic cyclic declines. The cougar, like the plains wolf and the plains grizzly, was once a regular prairie resident. Now it is extremely rare, represented by only the occasional wanderer from nearby forested areas.

A number of typically mountain or foothill mammals will occasionally be seen within the prairie coulees. Long-tailed mountain and red-backed voles, little northern chipmunks, bushy-tailed woodrats, red squirrels, Columbian and, northward, Franklin ground squirrels, timber wolves, wolverine, black bear, elk and moose might all, at one time or another, be glimpsed within the coulees of the south. Usually they are simply passing through en route to adjacent mountainous or forested regions but, in areas of marginal habitat adjacent to their normal ranges, some will become semi-permanent coulee residents.

the seasons

UNLIKE THE USUAL CALENDAR YEAR of winter, spring, summer and autumn, to a biotic community early and late spring and early and late summer are each as distinctive as autumn and winter. The six representative seasons then, are winter, early spring, late spring, early summer, late summer and autumn.

In winter, the prairie community is reduced and simplified; for many prairie species, it is a time of retreat beneath the surface of the grassland. Amphibians and reptiles have vanished, the toads into some easily dug sand deposit, the frogs buried in the muddy bottoms of prairie ponds. The snakes have disappeared into rocky crevices or usurped the burrows of ground squirrels, perhaps already enlarged and then abandoned by an industrious badger. Scores of lower animals have burrowed deep within the earth; the larvae of May beetles may be at depths of 100 centimetres or more, harvester ants as deep as two to three metres, descending below the normal frost line. Enduring frost and unharmed by desiccation, the eggs deposited within a few centimetres of the soil surface by the previous summer's crop of grasshoppers overwinter viable and unharmed. Others, the crickets and spiders, ants and ground beetles, have sought refuge in the thick basal tufts of the perennial grasses (Costello, p. 34).

From mid-December through February, the quiet cold of winter dominates the coulee landscapes (*plate 37*). Between coulees, the windswept prairie appears barren and desolate. The only evidence of life are the trails broken through the crusted snow by deer moving from one coulee to the next, or the tramplings of pronghorn and cattle moving about to feed. The only movement is that of the small seed-eating birds, the snow-buntings and, in mild winters, the Lapland longspur, species which have migrated south from their arctic nesting areas to winter on the shortgrass prairie, feeding on the standing heads of forbs and grasses. More common winter residents are the grey-crowned rosy finches and horned larks which have descended eastward off the alpine meadows.

Finally, each winter reaches its quota of blizzards and chinooks and the April prevernal (early spring) arrives with its first signs of the season's transition. Brown, muddy earth begins to appear along the icy rim of snowbanks. The earliest tiny plants probe upwards, pussy willows appear, and magpies begin fussing more than usual. Often, the first crocuses disappear beneath a last late snow but the days lengthen into a week of sunshine and victory goes to the flowers. To the west, the mountains are still white-capped. It will be well into summer before there is more dark than light on their distant slopes.

However hesitant, no observer can long resist the coming of spring. All must ultimately succumb to the unity of earth and meadowlarks and soaring hawks. By mid-April the earliest spring-returning birds are back; millions of tiny wildflowers have begun thrusting their way out of the earth, as rapidly as winter retreats. With true spring, the green of the coulee's new growth dominates the view. The shortest of the showy forbs arrive and blossom while the green shoots of plants that will bloom in summer and autumn find shelter for their new beginnings beneath those already established (*plates 38, 39*). The grasses are dominant, a backdrop to the rest, but the showy flowered forbs are the ones that colorfully identify the seasonal changes of prairie and coulee. Though varying with altitude and latitude, in each area the forbs bloom in orderly progression, generally those "in season" increasing in height as the growing period progresses.

Insects are perhaps the creatures best attuned to the season's floral progression. The variety of insect-plant relationships is phenomenal. Some chew leaves, some suck the juices from leaves and stems, some are pollen feeders and others live on roots beneath the ground. Though the relationships between plants and insects are rarely simple, their complexity and variety are increased further by the complex nature of insect life cycles, various stages of which may be spent in surroundings and under conditions, one quite different from the other. The larval or other pre-adult forms of a particular insect may be of a completely different nature than the adult, as is the moth or butterfly from its over-wintering pupa, and that, in turn, from its caterpillar. The duration of various stages of insect life cycles are equally varied. The May beetle, for example, spends three years as a root-chewing grub before transforming into a pupa and emerging as an adult in its fourth spring.

For each coulee insect, the time of seasonal abundance depends on the species and the characteristics of its individual life cycle. Some species feed on seeds, others on dead insects. Because of their lack of dependence on green foliage, certain ants are among the first insects to appear in spring. Others, such as the aphid-tending honey-gathering ants, only become active after their aphid stock begins to provide the honeydew used by the ants for food (Costello, p. 30).

Insects of one type or another occupy every conceivable environment within the coulee, each stage of each species filling its own special niche. Some, like the springtails, dwell beneath decaying vegetation while aphids, grasshoppers (*plate 41*), spittlebugs, and countless other insects are found on the leaves of grasses and forbs. In and around the coulee ponds are dragonflies, mosquitoes and their larvae and a variety of water beetles. Stoneflies, mayflies, damselflies and caddiceflies build their nests on the rocks and vegetation of the prairie streams. Crickets and seventeen-year cicadas with their shovel-like forelegs are in the soil along with excavators like the ground beetles and hunting wasps which deposit their eggs on the corpses of captive spiders to provide food for the developing larvae. Some insects deposit their eggs in the fresh droppings of grazing animals while every vertebrate has its dependent parasites. The tremendous number of flies, ants, bees and wasps are found everywhere.

By early summer the bluestems and other grasses have overcropped the spring flowers. Profuse numbers of species and patterns of vegetation characterize the coulees; golden beans, white and purple clovers and a variety of colorful daisies each in turn provide a hillside show.

The prairie is characterized by a multi-layering of species. As the older plants produce seeds and become senescent, colorful new and taller components are added, always against the background of the grasses. In dry years, drought may cause a shortening of the growing season with a resultant overlap of the flowering of species which would normally blossom in sequence. In such years, autumn species may flower in June.

The reptiles and amphibians of the coulee are most active during mid-summer (*plate 40*). On the top of a sandstone cliff in a coulee near Writing-On-Stone Provincial Park, there is a den of rattlesnakes (*plate 42*): it is beneath a rocky ledge, just where the downward slope of buffalo and spear grass meets the sheer drop of the coulee wall.

Sometime after mid-April and before late September, it is best to be careful where you place your feet. Quietly resting in neat coils within the patches of creeping juniper or slowly draping along the sandstone ledges are dozens of prairie rattlers, some less than 30 cm long, others, adults, reaching nearly one and a half metres. In spring, there may still be a bullsnake and a garter snake or two, lingering awhile before they disperse to increasing distances as the summer progresses. By mid-summer the place is vacant, the snakes absent until the shorter days and cooler temperatures of autumn bring them together once more.

Unable to regulate their body temperatures by panting, perspiring, or by altering the insulating value of their body covering, amphibians and reptiles are almost totally dependent on the changing temperatures of their surroundings. During hot summer days their movements are limited to the morning and evening hours. The prairie rattlesnake, the egg-laying plains hognose snake, the bullsnake and the different species of plains garter snakes all seek sanctuary from the midday sun by moving underground or beneath the cooling cover of moist vegetation. Others, like the tiger salamander and the spadefoot toad, spend much of their adult life underground in burrows, emerging to breed only at night and only during spring or summer rains. Like the ant-eating eastern short-horned lizard, or "horned toad," these last are almost always found near loose, sandy or gravelly soil suitable for burrowing.

Long dry periods typify the semi-arid grasslands in mid-summer. The occasional thunderstorm serves only to postpone the inevitable desiccation which will accompany autumn and winter. The sloughs gradually diminish in size. By August, a large portion of their clay bottoms are exposed, to harden and crack in the sun (*plate 43*). In the coulees, if there is water the green of the vegetation remains, oasis-like. If not, the heat reflected from the yellowing slopes will sear and dry the plants. Too long without moisture and the shrivelled plants begin to expose the soil beneath them in ever-increasing amounts. On the prairie above the coulee, the green fades earlier; by late summer much is crushed and trampled by the hooves of grazing stock.

In most years, by November virtually all plant growth above ground has halted. Only the annuals actually die, a small percentage of the total number of prairie plant species. Though quiescent, most of the prairie plants, perennials, live through the winter, surviving on food substances translocated to underground bulbs and roots the previous summer and autumn.

Above ground, the desiccated leaves and stems form a protective blanket over the prairie sod, retarding erosion and the loss of soil moisture essential for the spring regrowth. Those portions not utilized for winter forage by the prairie herbivores will be used by the plant in spring to augment the nutrients stored underground. When the next growth period arrives, most grasses will transmit organic substances back from the leaves and stems that are still attached to the growing parts. Little, if any, of the litter and debris of winter vegetation is wasted. Virtually all is re-used, ultimately, by the countless micro-organisms and invertebrates to begin again the dynamic processes of the ecosystem.

epilogue

PERHAPS SPECIAL PLACES exist only in the minds of the observers, the special places where the human spirit joins freely to the movement of the land, where happiness within is expressed in the beauty without.

East of the town of Milk River, Alberta, near Writing-On-Stone Provincial Park, there is such a place (*figure 12*). It is a coulee, sandstone rimmed with a spring-fed creek meandering through the bottom. Along the edge of the stream are poplars, birches and large, old, peach-leaved willows. There too are impenetrable thickets where porcupines, mice, bobcats and cottontails find refuge; where whitetail and mule deer have worn a maze of brushy tunnels through which a man can pass only on hands and knees.

All along the cliffs are the dens of yellow-bellied marmots. A few great horned owls and fewer prairie falcons nest in hollows wind-carved from the cliff faces. Ferruginous hawk nests are common on the ledges and pinnacles, some great cones of twigs and assembled debris achieving heights of one and two metres. Many are no longer used but in most years, at least one pair returns to rear its young. Sparrow hawks nest in small cliff-face cavities, or next door to flickers, in the decaying trunk of an old cottonwood. Lower, in more out-of-the-wind shrubbery, Swainson hawks, warblers and thrushes build their homes.

They are small and they are hidden, but there are prairie places yet wild and remote, another world beneath the level of the grass in which bits and pieces of a lost wilderness may still be found. With sensitivity and stewardship, they will remain.

---

figure 12, previous page: Van Cleeve coulee

Glossary

ACCIPITER. Any hawk of the genus *Accipiter*, characterized by short wings and a long tail

BIOGEOGRAPHY. The biological study of the geographical distribution of plants and animals

BIOMASS. The total mass of living organisms in a given habitat

BIOME. The largest geographical community unit (e.g. tundra, tropical rain forest, temperate grassland, desert), with similar life forms and environmental conditions

BIOTIC COMMUNITY. Any assemblage of populations living in a prescribed area or physical habitat

BUTEO. Any of various hawks of the genus *Buteo*, heavily built hawks characterized by broad, rounded wings and broad, rounded tails

ECOSYSTEM. The system resulting from all of the interactions of the plant and animal communities, functioning together with the non-living environment

ECOTONE. A zone of transition or junction between two or more diverse biotic communities

EDGE EFFECT. The tendency for increased variety and density at community junctions.

FORB. Any herb that is not a grass or sedge

HERB. Any plant with no permanent parts above the ground, as distinct from shrubs and trees

PERMEANT. A highly mobile animal which links or couples biologically diverse communities and ecological subsystems by being able to move freely between them, e.g. birds, mammals and flying insects

RAPTOR. A bird of prey

bibliography

Allen, Durward L. 1967. *The Life of Prairies and Plains*. McGraw-Hill Book Company.

Banfield, A.W.F. 1974. *The Mammals of Canada*. University of Toronto Press for National Museum of Natural Sciences, National Museums of Canada.

Beaty, C.B. 1975a. *Coulee Alignment and The Wind in Southern Alberta, Canada*. Bulletin, Geological Society of America, Vol. 86, No. 1, pp. 119-128.

Beaty, C.B. 1975b. *The Landscapes of Southern Alberta: A Regional Geomorphology*. The University of Lethbridge Production Services, 98 pp., illus.

Budd, Archibald C. and Keith F. Best. 1964. *Wild Plants of the Canadian Prairies*. Queen's Printer, Ottawa.

Cormack, R.G.H. 1967. *Wild Flowers of Alberta*. The Queen's Printer, Edmonton.

Costello, David F. 1969. *The Prairie World*. Thomas Y. Crowell Company, New York. xiv + 242 pp.

Godfrey, W. Earl. 1966. *The Birds of Canada*. Queen's Printer, Ottawa.

Hardy, W.C. et al. 1967. *Alberta - A Natural History*. M.G. Hurtig, Edmonton.

Kendeigh, S.C. 1961. *Animal Ecology*. Prentice-Hall Inc. Englewood Cliffs, N.J. 468 pp.

Kuijt, Job. 1972. *Common Coulee Plants of Southern Alberta*. The University of Lethbridge Production Services. xiv + 130 pp., illus.

Leopold, Aldo. 1949. *A Sand County Almanac and Sketches Here and There*. Oxford University Press.

Lewin, V. 1963. *The Herpetofauna of Southeastern Alberta*. Can. Field-Nat. 77:203-214.

McAllister, D.E. and E.J. Crossman. 1973. *A Guide to the Freshwater Sport Fishes of Canada*. National Museum of Natural Sciences Natural History Series, No. 1. National Museums of Canada.

Odum, Eugene P. 1971. *Fundamentals of Ecology, Third Edition*. W.B. Saunders Company, Philadelphia. xiv + 574 pp.

Paetz, Martin J. and J.S. Nelson. 1970. *The Fishes of Alberta*. The Queen's Printer, Edmonton.

Rodney, William. 1969. *Kootenai Brown: His Life and Times*. Gray's Publishing Ltd. 251 pp.

Salt, W. Ray and A.L. Wilk. 1958. *The Birds of Alberta*. Hamly Press Ltd., Edmonton.

Scott, W.B. and E.J. Crossman. 1973. *Freshwater Fishes of Canada*. Bulletin 184, Fisheries Research Board of Canada, Ottawa.

Soper, J. Dewey. 1964. *The Mammals of Alberta*. The Hamly Press Ltd., Edmonton.

Stegner, Wallace. 1955. *Wolf Willow*. The Viking Press, New York.

index

About the Author

Thomas Willock, raised in shortgrass prairie coulee country along the Alberta-Montana border, is best known for his powerful photographic images of western wildlife. His photographs and writings have been published in Canada, the U.S.A. and Europe. A zoologist and a natural history photojournalist, he received his B.Sc. from the University of Alberta and his M.Sc. from Carleton University, Ottawa. Since 1978, he has served as Director of the Medicine Hat Museum and Art Gallery.